CRANES

PICTURE LIBRARY

CRANES

R. J. Stephen

Franklin Watts

London New York Sydney Toronto

© 1986 Franklin Watts Ltd

First published in Great Britain
  1986 by
Franklin Watts Ltd
12a Golden Square
London W1R 4BA

First published in the USA by
Franklin Watts Inc
387 Park Avenue South
New York
N.Y. 10016

First published in Australia by
Franklin Watts
14 Mars Road
Lane Cove
2066 NSW

UK ISBN: 0 86313 399 1
US ISBN: 0–531–10183–5
Library of Congress Catalog Card
Number 85–42089

Printed in Italy
by Tipolitografia G. Canale & C. S.p.A. - Turin

Designed by
Barrett & Willard

Photographs by
Central Electricity Generating Board
Grove Coles Cranes
Heerema/Bob Fleumer
Kato Cranes UK
Liebherr Great Britain
Mansell Collection
Geoff Mead
OCL
Royal Ordnance
Sparrows Crane Hire
Stothert & Pitt
Taylor Woodrow
NEI Thompson
UK Land Forces HQ
ZEFA

Illustration by
Rhoda and Robert Burns

Technical Consultant
Geoff Mead

Series Editor
N. S. Barrett

Contents

Introduction

Cranes are machines used to lift and move heavy objects. They are used in such places as construction sites, docks, factories, warehouses and railways.

Most cranes are driven by electric or diesel motors. They work by a system of pulleys. Some cranes are called derricks or hoists.

△ A truck-mounted crane lifts a heavy load from a trailer. The crane operator can just be seen in his cab at the back.

Most cranes are mobile. They can move about under their own power. Truck cranes, traveling cranes and crawler cranes are examples of mobile cranes. Truck cranes are mounted on wheeled carriers and crawler cranes on tracks.

Derricks are usually fixed, but can be turned to cover large areas.

△ The large cranes are traveling cranes. They move along tracks on the dock and unload containers from the ship. The smaller cranes on the ship are derricks.

The traveling crane

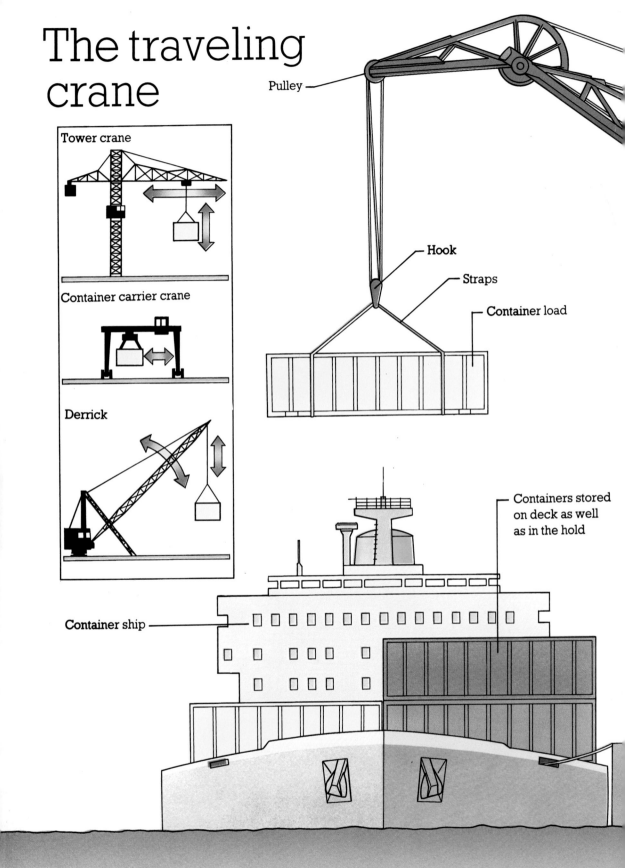

Tower crane

Container carrier crane

Derrick

Pulley

Hook

Straps

Container load

Containers stored
on deck as well
as in the hold

Container ship

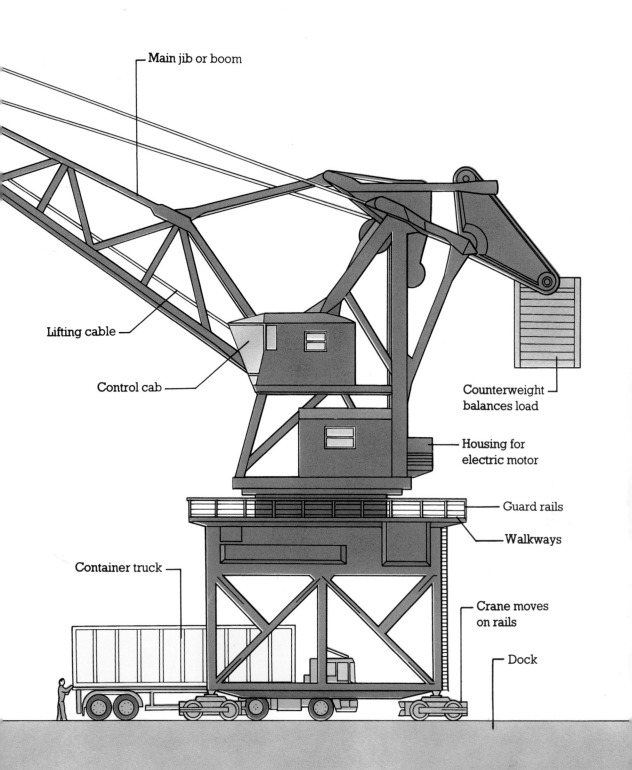

Main jib or boom

Lifting cable

Control cab

Container truck

Counterweight balances load

Housing for electric motor

Guard rails

Walkways

Crane moves on rails

Dock

9

Operating a crane

Operating a crane requires great skill. The operator sits in a cab with foot and hand controls. In some cranes, the operator's cab is at the top, high above the ground.

Cranes are fitted with many safety devices and there are warning lights in the cab. The movements of the crane can be restricted within certain limits. Brakes come on automatically if the power fails.

▷ The operator of a crawler crane has hand and foot controls. There are different controls for propelling the crawler, for swinging the cab and crane around and for working the crane.

▽ The inside of a crane cab on an offshore oil rig. The controls and operator's seat are designed for maximum comfort and efficiency.

Truck cranes

Truck cranes come in all sizes and are used for many different types of work. One of the simplest is the tow truck, which has a crane to hoist up one end of a vehicle for towing.

The biggest truck cranes can lift weights of 1,100 tons (1,000 mt) or more. Some have telescopic booms, which extend to heights of over 415 ft (130 m).

△ A large truck crane on its way to the next job. It has several sets of wheels and axles to bear the weight of the crane while on the road.

▷ The crane in action, lifting a heavy tower into place. This crane can lift weights up to 550 tons (500 mt). The outriggers, or stabilizing legs, give it a very firm base.

◁ A bird's-eye view of a truck crane lifting a heavy piece of machinery.

▷ An excavator fitted with a special grab for lifting scrap metal.

▽ Teamwork: four truck-mounted cranes cooperate to lift a metal roof structure.

Fixed cranes

Most tower cranes are fixed. They are often used in the construction of high-rise buildings. Some can reach across as much as 180 ft (55 m) to carry materials to workers on top.

A derrick is a fixed crane in which the boom is supported at the back by a vertical mast or other structure. The boom is hinged near the bottom of the mast.

▽ Tower cranes on the construction sites of power stations (below and below left). Tower cranes take up little ground space. The boom sticks out from the top of the tower to reach its loads. The hook is suspended from a trolley that runs along the boom. There are weights on the back of the boom to balance the loads.

◁ A ship's derrick in action. The boom is supported by cables attached to a mast.

▽ Tower cranes stretch up toward the sky, and special extensions give them extra reach.

◁ Tower cranes ring an oil platform under construction in the sea. These enormous offshore structures are built up with parts and materials brought from sites on land.

Traveling cranes

Traveling cranes run along tracks, overhead or on the ground. Overhead cranes are sometimes called bridge cranes. They move back and forth on overhead rails. They are used chiefly in factories and workshops.

Cranes running on ground tracks are found at docksides and in railroad yards. They may be used for loading and unloading freight, containers and machinery.

▽ A traveling crane runs on rails over the production line of a factory making tanks. The operator of this bridge crane can be seen in the cab on the left. He can raise or lower the load and can move the hoisting machinery back and forth along the rails of the bridge.

△ Traveling cranes
running on rails can
load and unload
containers directly on to
and from trains.

◁ Traveling cranes run
along special tracks on
the dock. They transfer
containers directly from
trucks to the container
ship or from ship to
truck.

21

Crawler cranes

Crawler cranes are mobile cranes mounted on steel tracks. They provide a heavy base for the crane. They can travel over rough and uneven ground but the lifting area must be flat.

One advantage of crawlers is that they can move about while carrying heavy loads. Some crawlers can "walk" with loads of 550 tons (500 mt) or more.

△ Crawler cranes are mounted on sturdy tracks. The cab and crane can swing round in a complete circle.

▷ A crawler crane lowers a support for a new highway into place.

Floating cranes

Floating cranes are used in docks and harbors. They are either self-propelled or mounted on pontoons, or platforms. They load and unload ships where there are no land-based cranes or when there are no loading bays available.

Huge floating cranes have been built for work at sea, on ships or as semisubmersible vessels.

▷ A floating crane mounted on a pontoon unloads containers from a ship and lowers them on to the dock. Ropes from the ship are used to steady the pontoon and control its movements.

▽ Special ship cranes such as this one are capable of lifting very heavy loads at sea.

▷ The two cranes on
this semisubmersible
crane vessel combine to
lower a section on to an
offshore oil rig under
construction. Cranes
such as these are
capable of lifting
heavier loads than any
other type of crane.
They are used for the
installation of offshore
oil and gas platforms.

The story of cranes

Pulling down

The first lifting devices were made by primitive peoples. It was natural to raise a load by standing above it and pulling it up with a rope or vine. But they found it easier to pass a rope over a branch of a tree and to pull downward. In this way, the first simple hoist was invented.

Treading up

Early lifting machines were powered by men. About 1,600 years ago, the Romans used slaves to work treadmills. A treadmill was a large wheel

which was kept turning by the slaves, who walked inside it – like pet animals in an exercise cage. The shaft of the wheel was connected to a drum. As this turned, it wound up a rope, which slowly raised the load.

After the fall of the Roman Empire, cranes were not used for building until about AD 1000.

△ A steam derrick of 1864 uses pulleys and chains to lift a boat.

Handling cargo

Cranes were used for handling cargo in the Middle Ages. There were cranes in ports in the 1300s and by 1600 about sixty were in use around Europe, chiefly in

△ A crane of the Middle Ages powered by treadmill.

England, the Netherlands and along the River Rhine.

Steam power

The use of cranes increased from the mid-1700s, with the growth of the Industrial Revolution in Europe. Steam power was used to drive cranes and hoisting machinery in docks, factories and mines from the mid-1800s.

△ The world's first truck-mounted crane in 1922.

△ A rail-mounted grab crane of the early 1890s.

Hydraulic power

Hydraulic power was first used to drive cranes in the docks in 1846. The first hydraulic cranes used water pressure. Modern ones use oil pressure.

Further developments

Electric-powered cranes and cranes running on rails came into use in the 1880s. The first truck-

mounted cranes appeared in the early 1920s. Gasoline and diesel engines were first used for powering cranes in the 1920s.

Cranes with telescopic booms first arrived in the late 1950s. Since then, cranes have become more and more powerful, with their capacity increasing from little more than 22 tons (20 mt) in the early 1950s to over 1,100 tons (1,000 mt). Floating cranes have been built to lift more than 5,500 tons (5,000 mt).

△ A modern variable counterweight crane mounted on rails. The weight at the back moves to balance the load.

Facts and records

Power at sea

The world's most powerful cranes are semisubmersible vessels used for work on offshore oil rigs. The *Balder*, a vessel owned by Heerema, a Swiss firm of marine contractors, has two cranes. Used together, these cranes lifted nearly 6,270 tons (5,700 mt) in raising a deck assembly from a transport barge on to the legs of a rig under construction.

△ The two giant cranes of the *Balder*, a semisubmersible crane vessel.

Single lift

A Gottwald MK1000 crane, with a lifting capacity of 1,100 tons (1,000 mt), set a record of 816 tons (742 mt), the heaviest lift made by a single mobile crane. The record was set in New Zealand, when a reactor was lifted into place at a refinery.

△ The Gottwald MK 1000 crane (left), known as "Birdie One," during its record lift. Two large crawler cranes (right) were used to steady the base of the reactor.

Flying cranes

Helicopters often serve as lifting machines and some of them are called flying cranes. They are used for transporting heavy or awkward loads to places that cannot be reached by other means, such as the top of a dam or a very high building. Most transport helicopters cannot lift more than a few tons.

△ A helicopter about to lift a jeep.

Glossary

Axle
Axles are the shafts that carry the wheels of a truck. They bear the weight of the vehicle.

Boom
The main arm of a crane.

Bridge crane
An overhead traveling crane.

Container
A large, standard-sized box used for carrying cargo. Containers are transported to and from special container ships by road or rail.

Counterweight
A block of material such as concrete or iron used to balance the weight of the load being lifted, especially when the crane is turning. On some tower cranes, the counterweight is situated on the rear end of the boom.

Derrick
Derricks are fixed cranes, supported from behind by ropes or cables usually attached to a mast or other structure.

Hoist
A type of fixed crane. Hoists usually hang above the load to be lifted, from a girder or an overhead track. Hand hoists are used in factories and workshops. Another type of hoist carries materials and passengers up the side of a building.

Jib
The boom, or arm, of a crane or derrick.

Outriggers
Legs used to stabilize a mobile crane when in use.

Pulleys
Devices used to change the direction of the pull on a rope or wire. For example, a pulley enables a weight to be lifted by pulling downward. It has a grooved wheel, called a sheave, on which the rope runs. By using combinations of pulleys, cranes can lift loads with less effort.

Telescopic crane
A crane with a boom that can be extended hydraulically, by means of cylinder rods and oil pressure.

Tower crane
A type of fixed crane with a boom that extends from the top of a tower.

Index